Pre-school
Maths 4-5

Rhona Whiteford

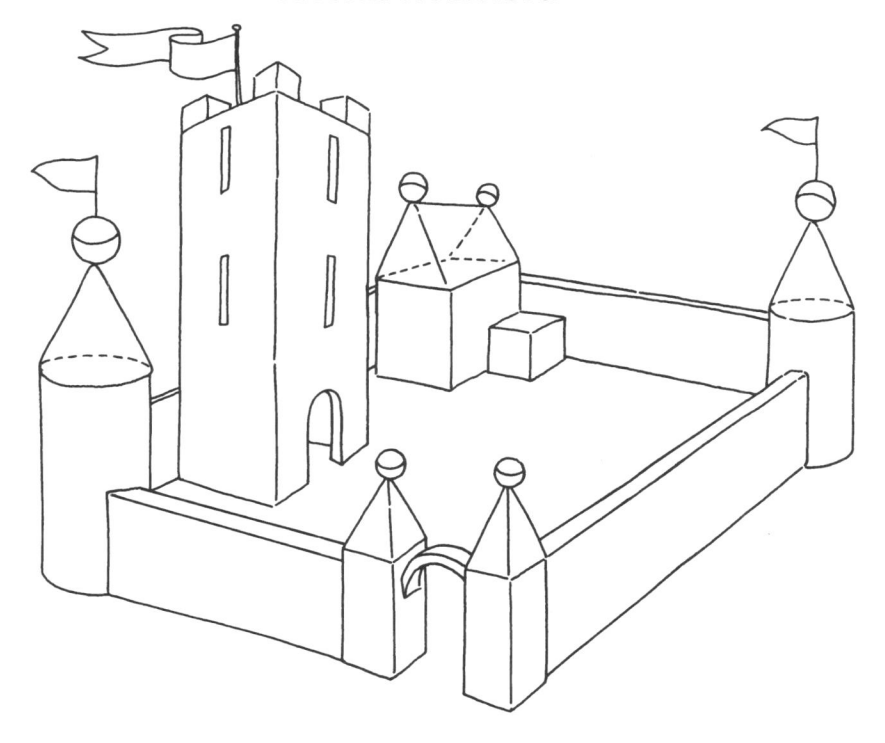

This book belongs to:

_____

WHSmith

Draw a set

Sorting shapes and colours

Draw a set of red lollipops.	Draw a set of green squares.
Draw a set of tall trees.	Draw a set of small stars.

Divide this set of fruit into four smaller sets.

Looking at a set

Dividing a set

This is a set of vehicles.
Draw a ring round the whole set. Then separate the different types with lines.

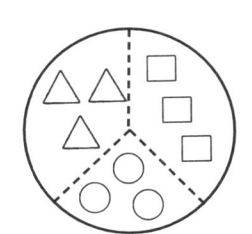

Colour your favourite type.
Which of these things have you been on?

3

Zero

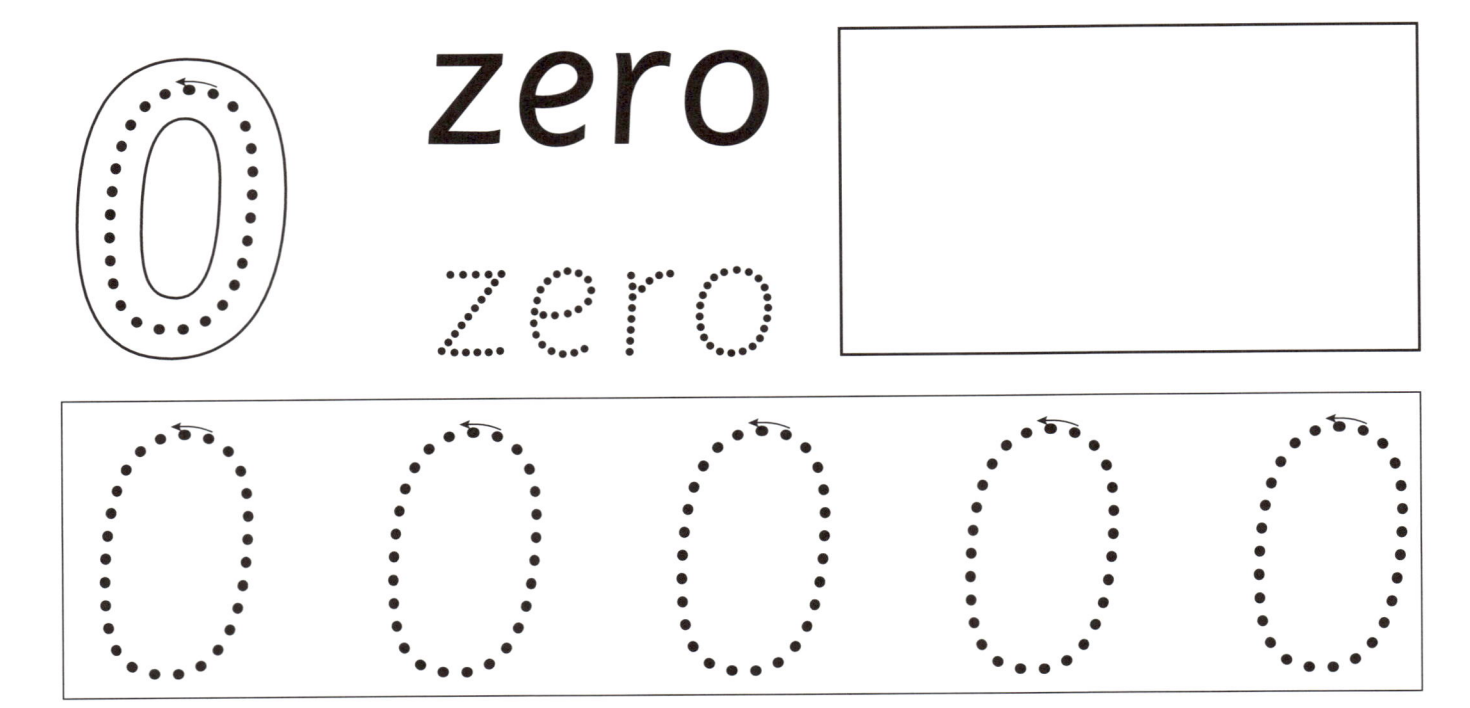

Recognising and writing numbers

zero

Zero is the number name for 'nothing'. Put a tick ✔ on the sets that have **0** in them.

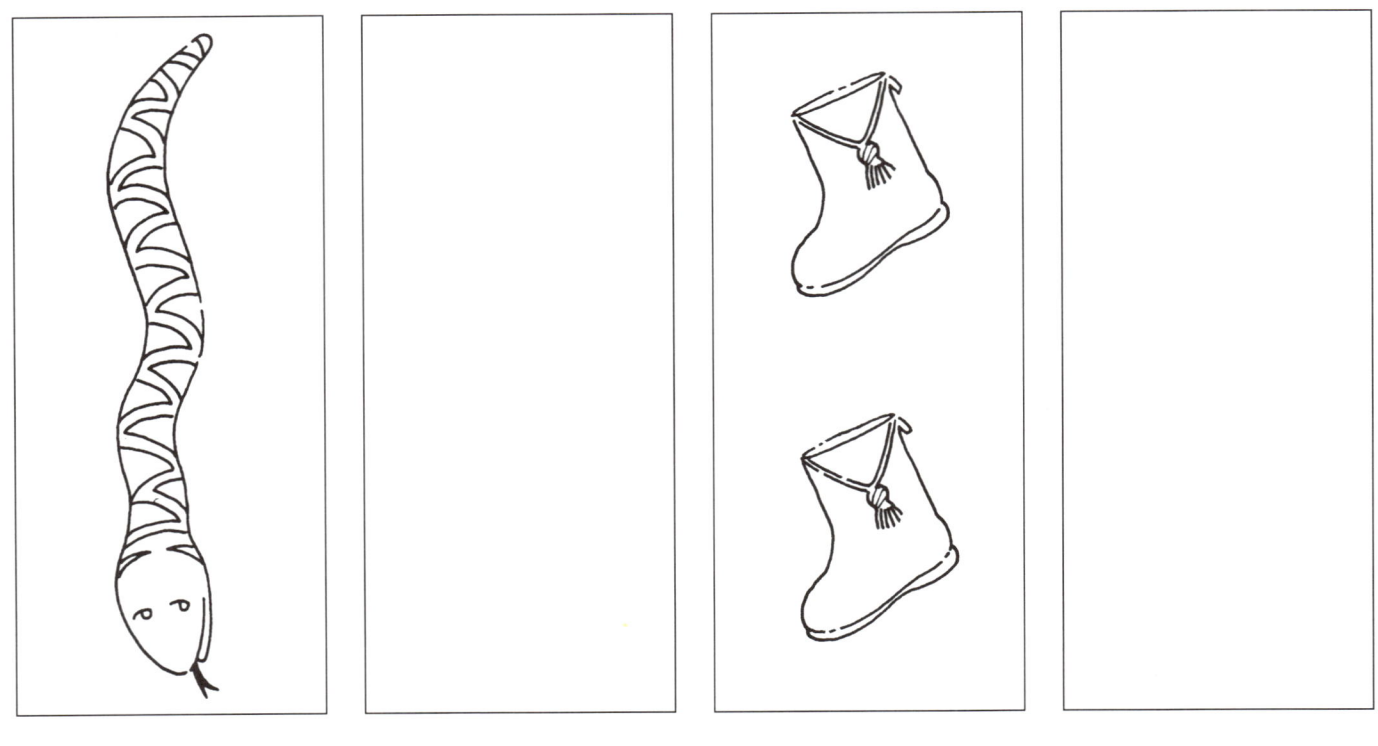

zero   zero   zero

Numbers 1–10

Recognising and writing numbers

one

one

Colour the set of **one**.
Then draw a set of **one** bucket.

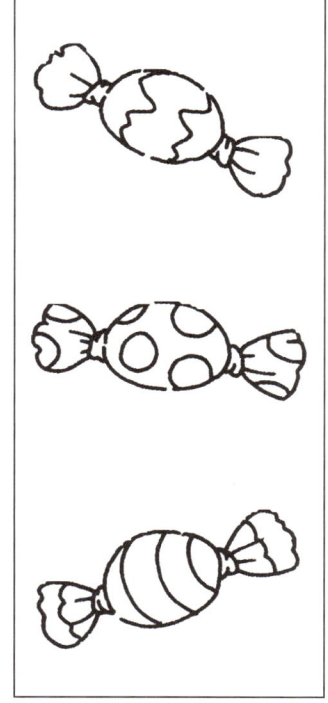

1 bucket

one   one   one

Numbers 1–10

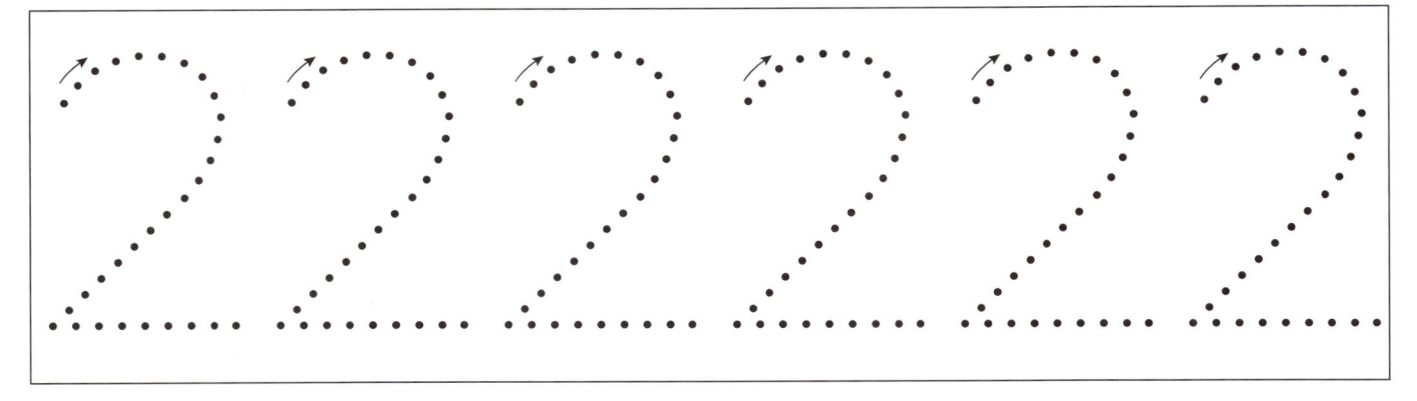

Recognising and writing numbers

2 two
two

2 2 2 2 2

Colour the set of **two**.
Then draw a set of **two** hats.

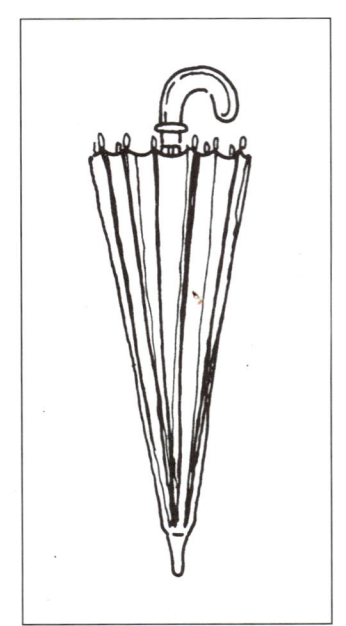

2 hats

two   two   two

Numbers 1–10

Recognising and writing numbers

3 three
three

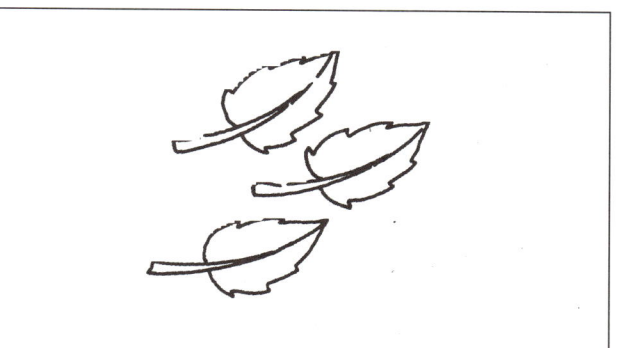

3 3 3 3 3 3

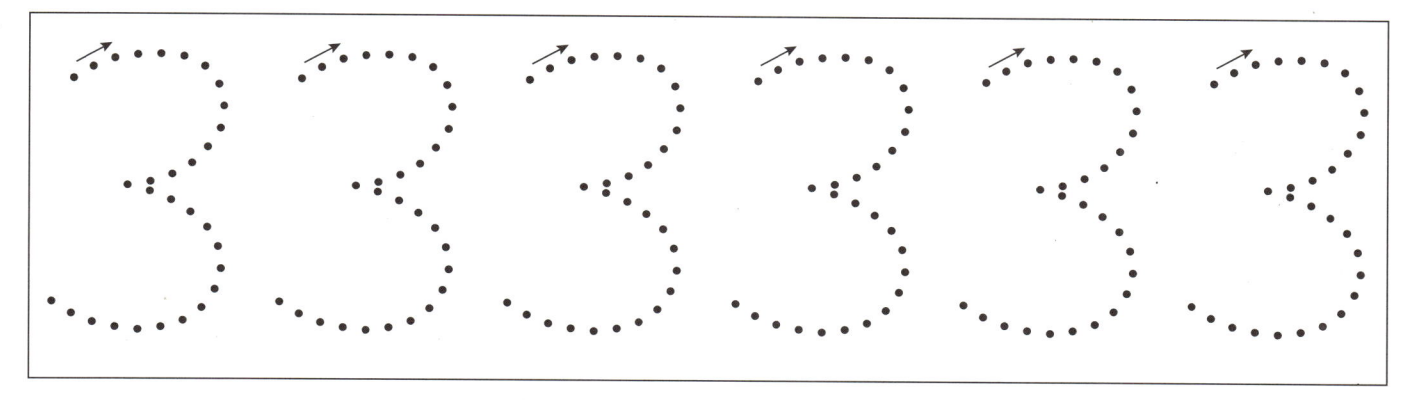

Colour the set of **three**.
Then draw a set of **three** bats.

3 bats

three three three

Numbers 1–10

Recognising and writing numbers

four
four

Colour the set of **four**.
Then draw a set of **four** cups.

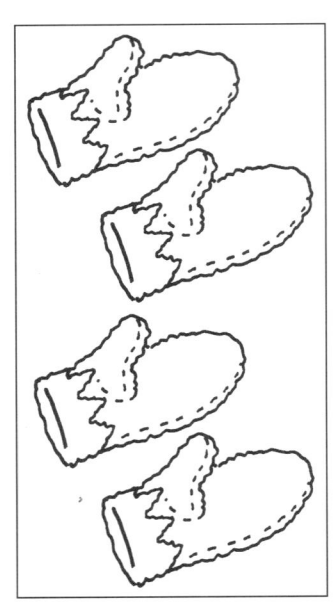

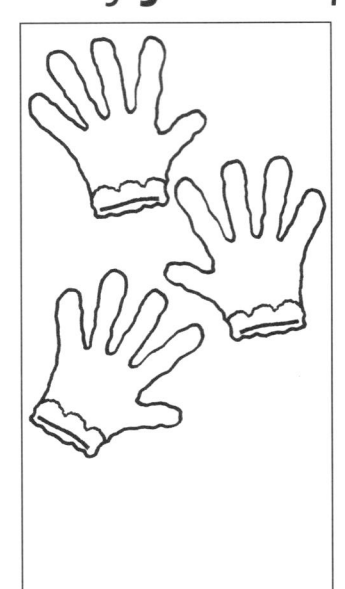

4 cups

four four four

8

Numbers 1–10

Recognising and writing numbers

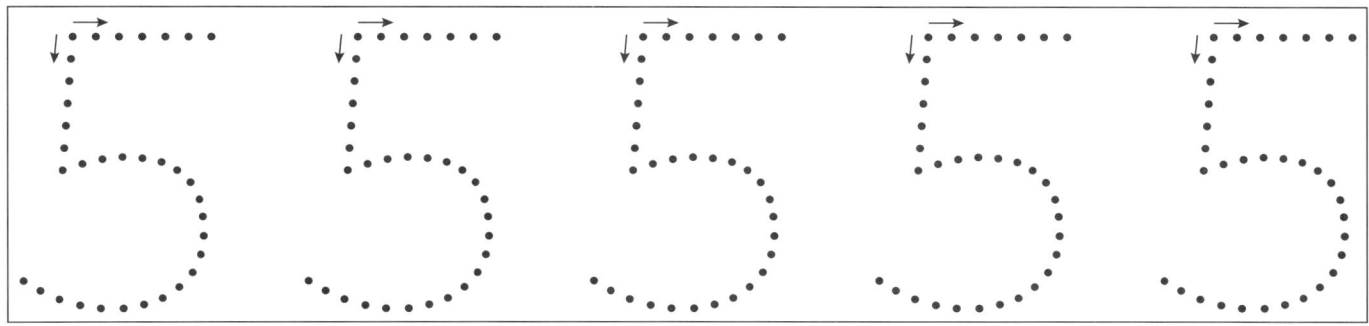

5 *five*

Colour the set of **five**.
Then draw a set of **five** cakes.

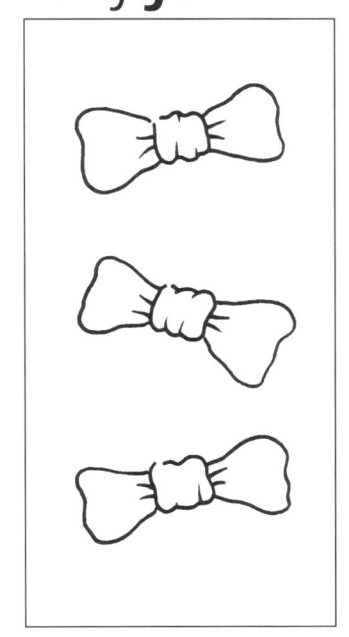

5 cakes

five   *five*   *five*

9

Numbers 1–10

Recognising and writing numbers

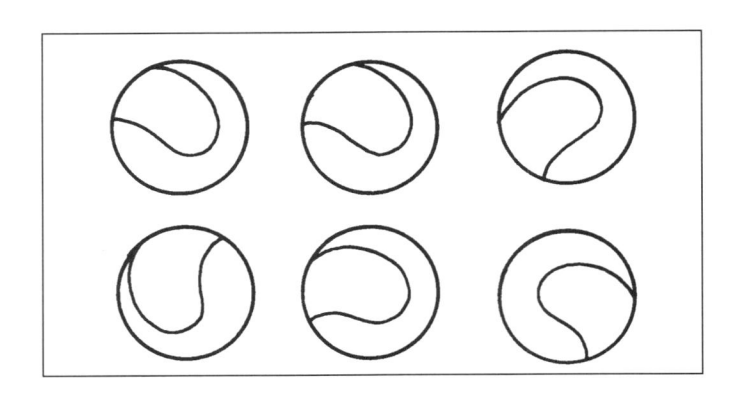

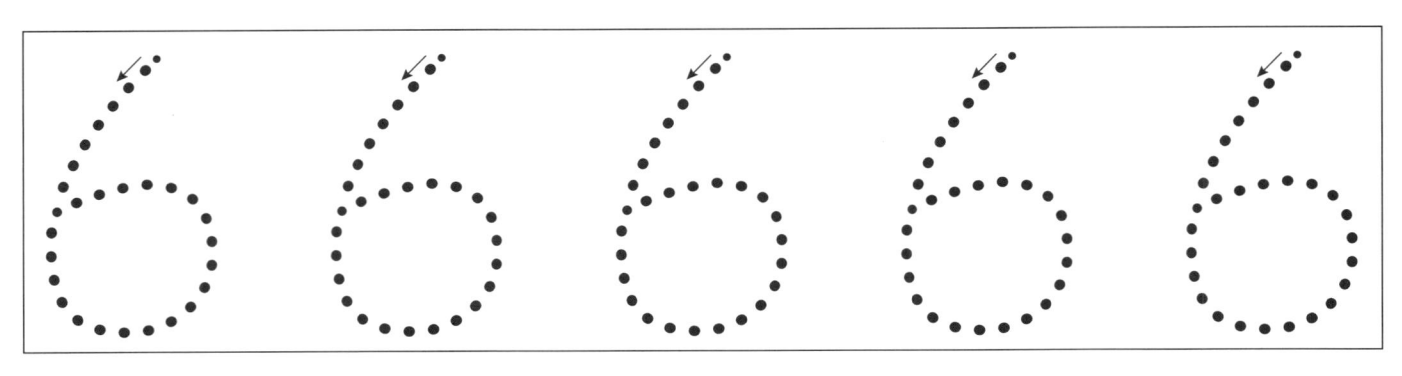

six

six

Colour the set of **six**.
Then draw a set of **six** oranges.

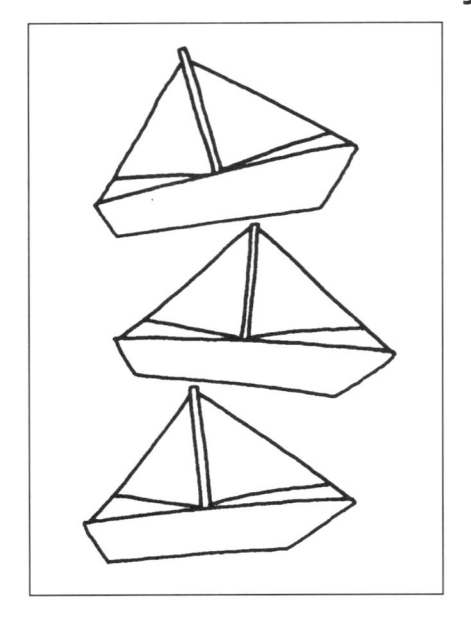

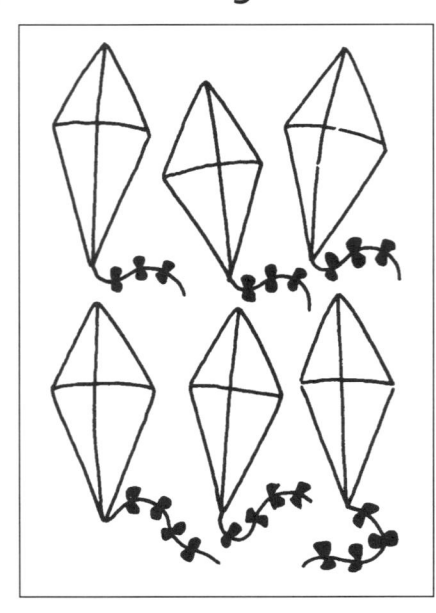

6 oranges

six   six   six

10

Numbers 1–10

Recognising and writing numbers

7 seven
seven

7 7 7 7 7

Colour the set of **seven**.
Then draw a set of **seven** pencils.

7 pencils

seven   seven

Numbers 1–10

Recognising and writing numbers

8 eight

eight

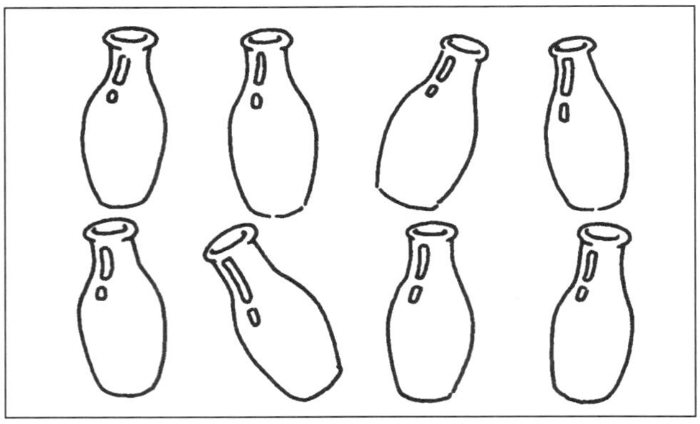

8 8 8 8 8

Colour the set of **eight**.
Then draw a set of **eight** apples.

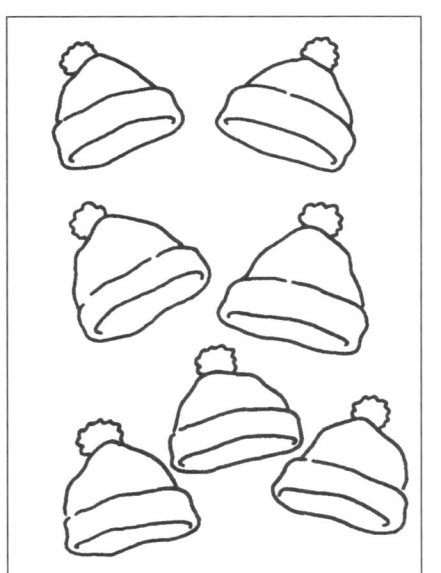

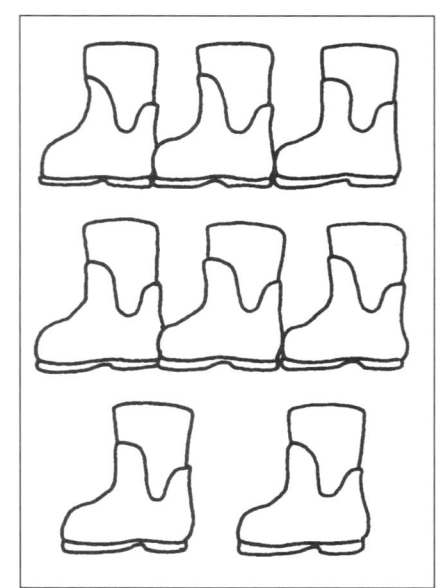

8 apples

eight eight

12

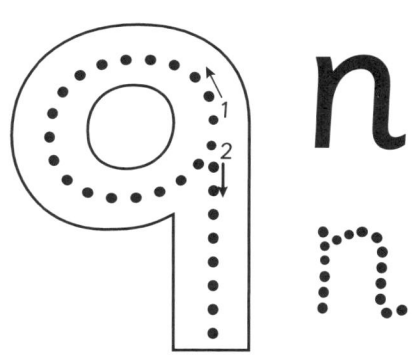

Numbers 1–10

Recognising and writing numbers

9 nine

nine

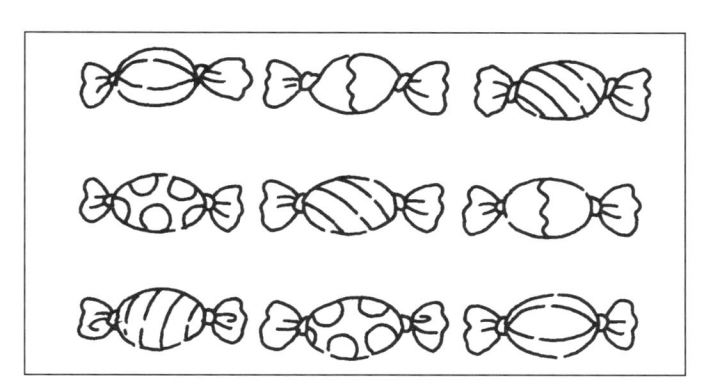

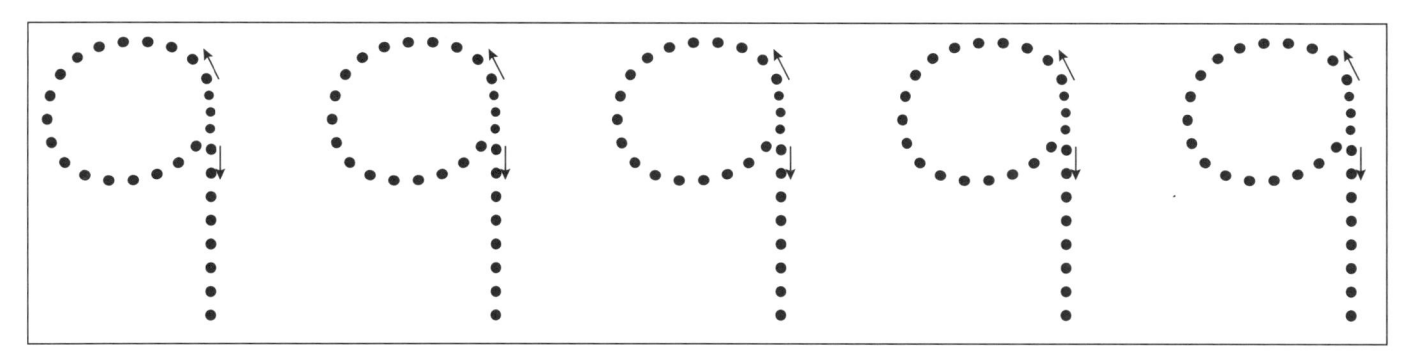

9 9 9 9 9

Colour the set of **nine**.
Then draw a set of **nine** books.

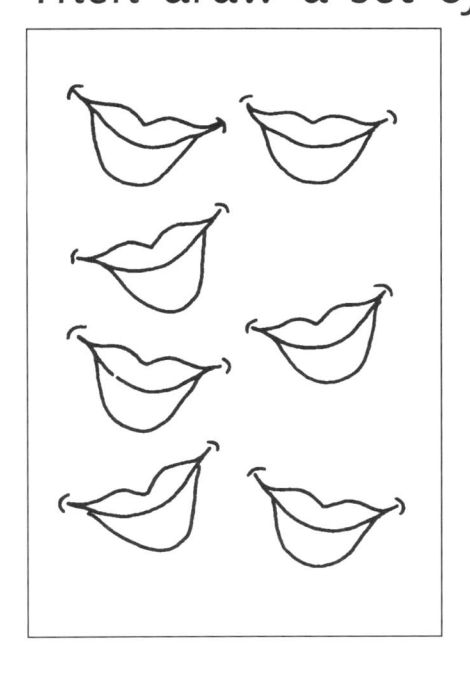

9 books

nine nine nine

Numbers 1–10

Recognising and writing numbers

10 ten
ten

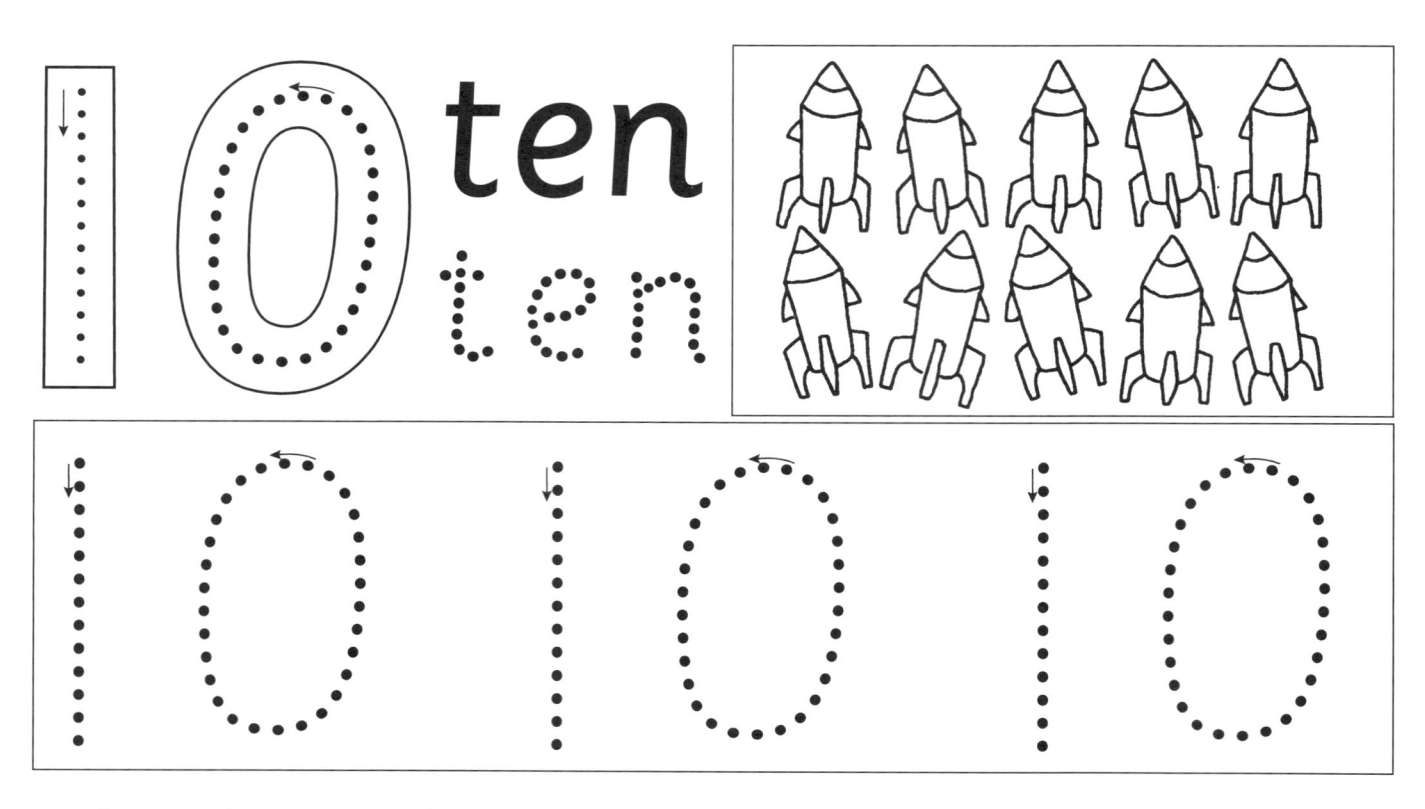

10 10 10

Colour the set of **ten**.
Then draw a set of **ten** bananas.

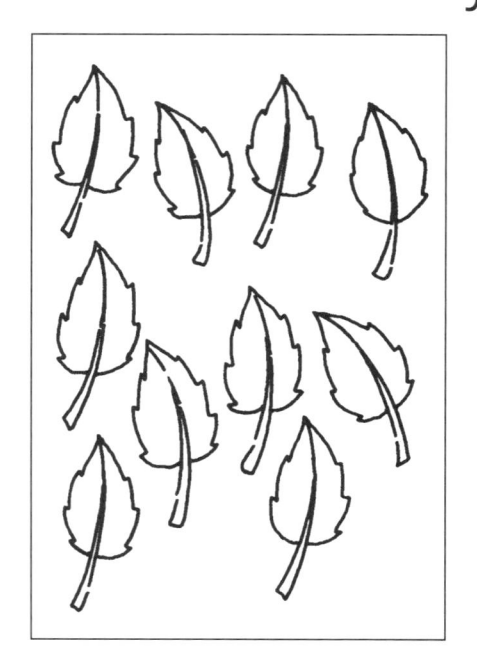

10 bananas

ten   ten   ten

14

Dot to dot 1–10

Following the order of numbers

| 1 | 2 | 3 | 4 | 5 | 6 | 7 | 8 | 9 | 10 |

What is mouse standing on? Join the dots to find out. Start at 1.

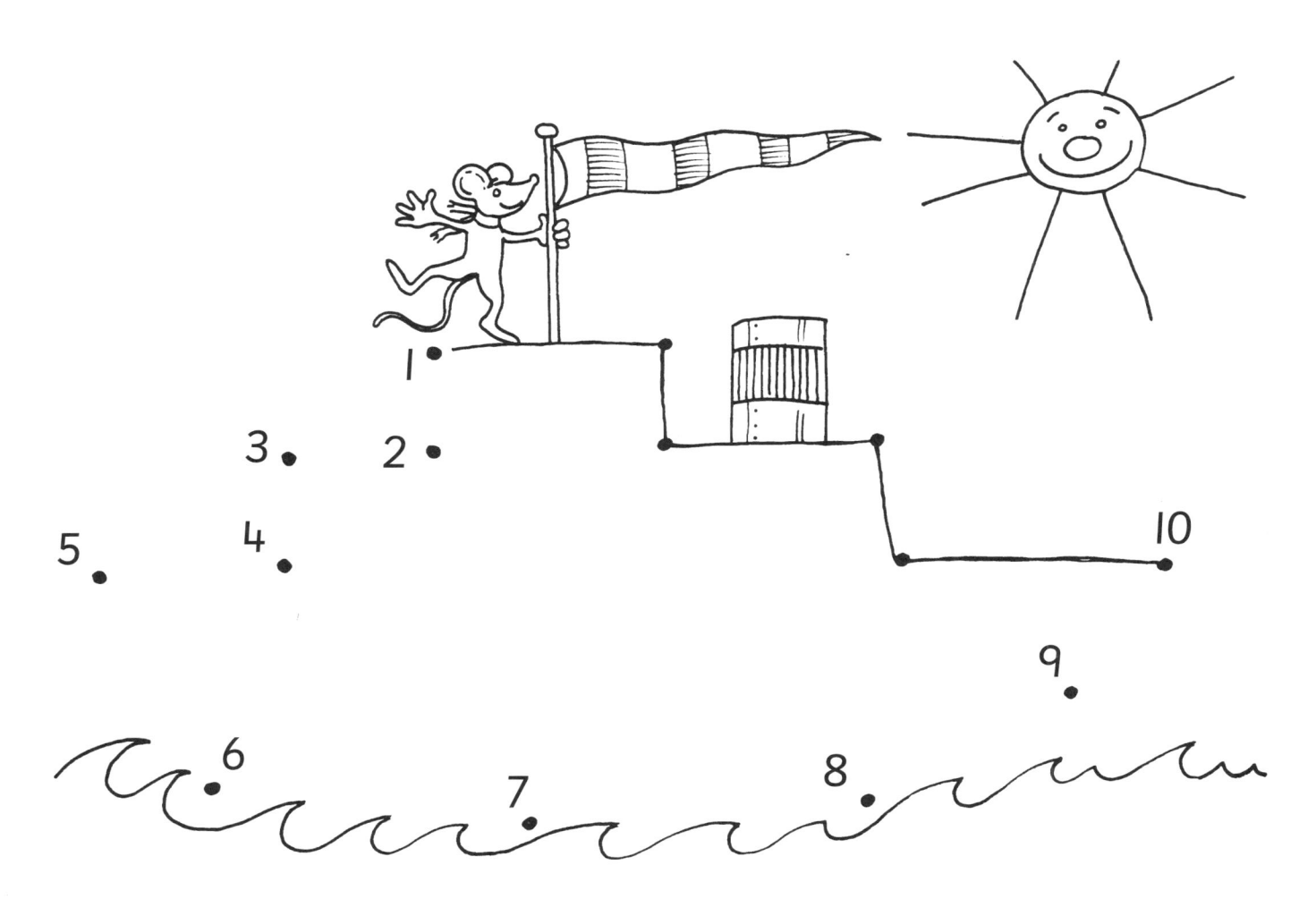

Draw another flag at the front of the boat.

Now there are _____ flags.

Parent Tip Language is very important to maths, so talk about the picture. e.g. ask 'Where is the mouse going?'

Number words

Recognising number words

Write the number and the word under each set.

1	2	3	4	5
one	two	three	four	five

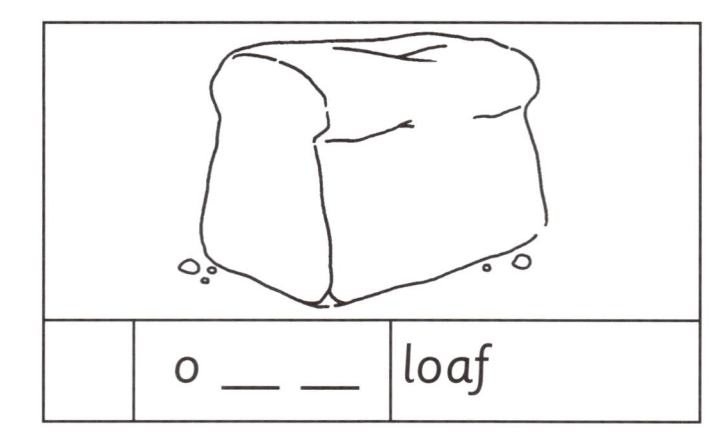

o _ _ loaf

t _ _ ices

t _ _ _ _ jellies

f _ _ _ cakes

f _ _ _ sweets

Number words

Recognising number words

Write the number and the word under each set.

6	7	8	9	10
six	seven	eight	nine	ten

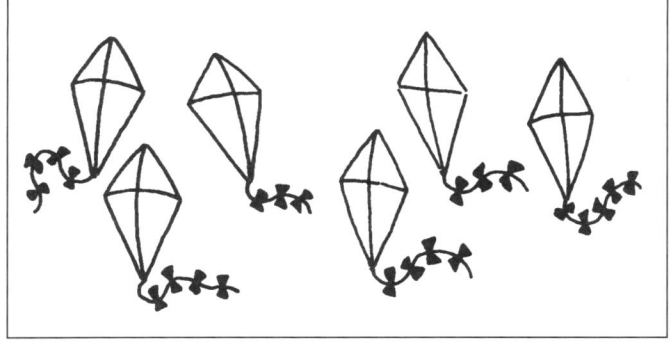

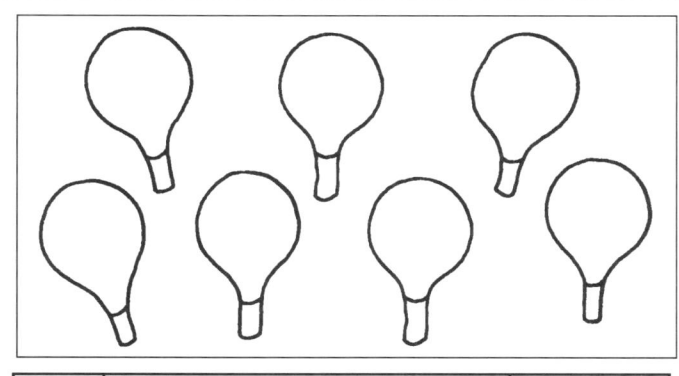

s _ _ kites

s _ _ _ _ bats

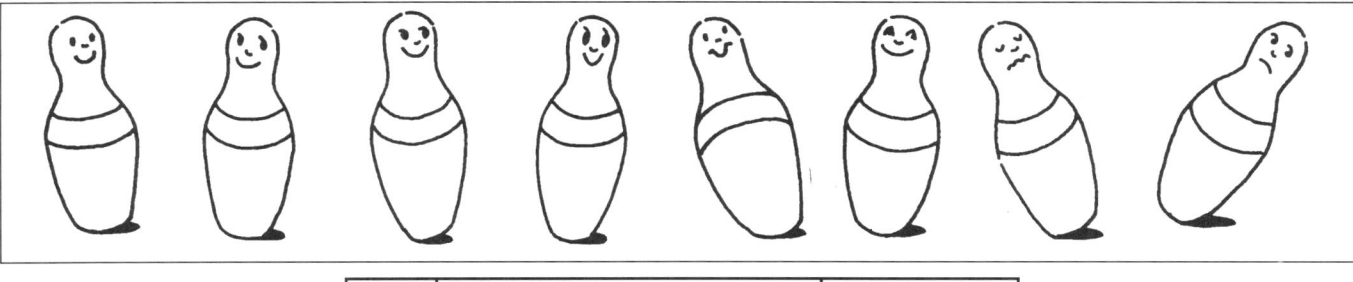

e _ _ _ _ skittles

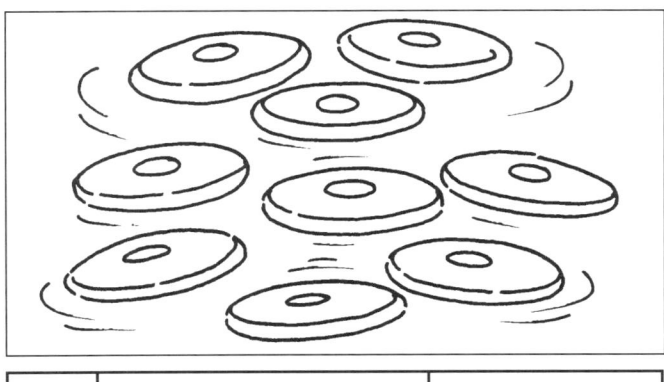

n _ _ _ frisbees

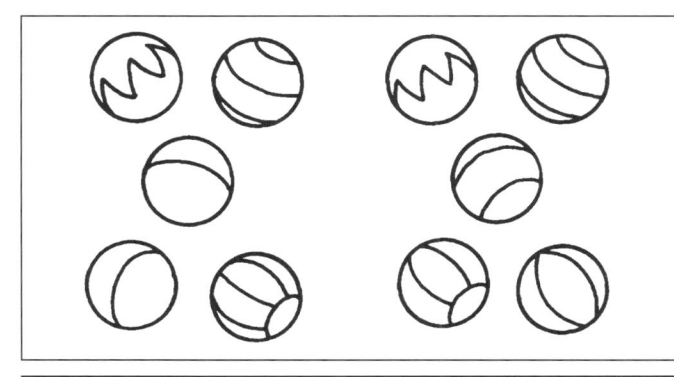

t _ _ balls

17

Draw and count

Making sets

Draw and colour the number of things in each set.

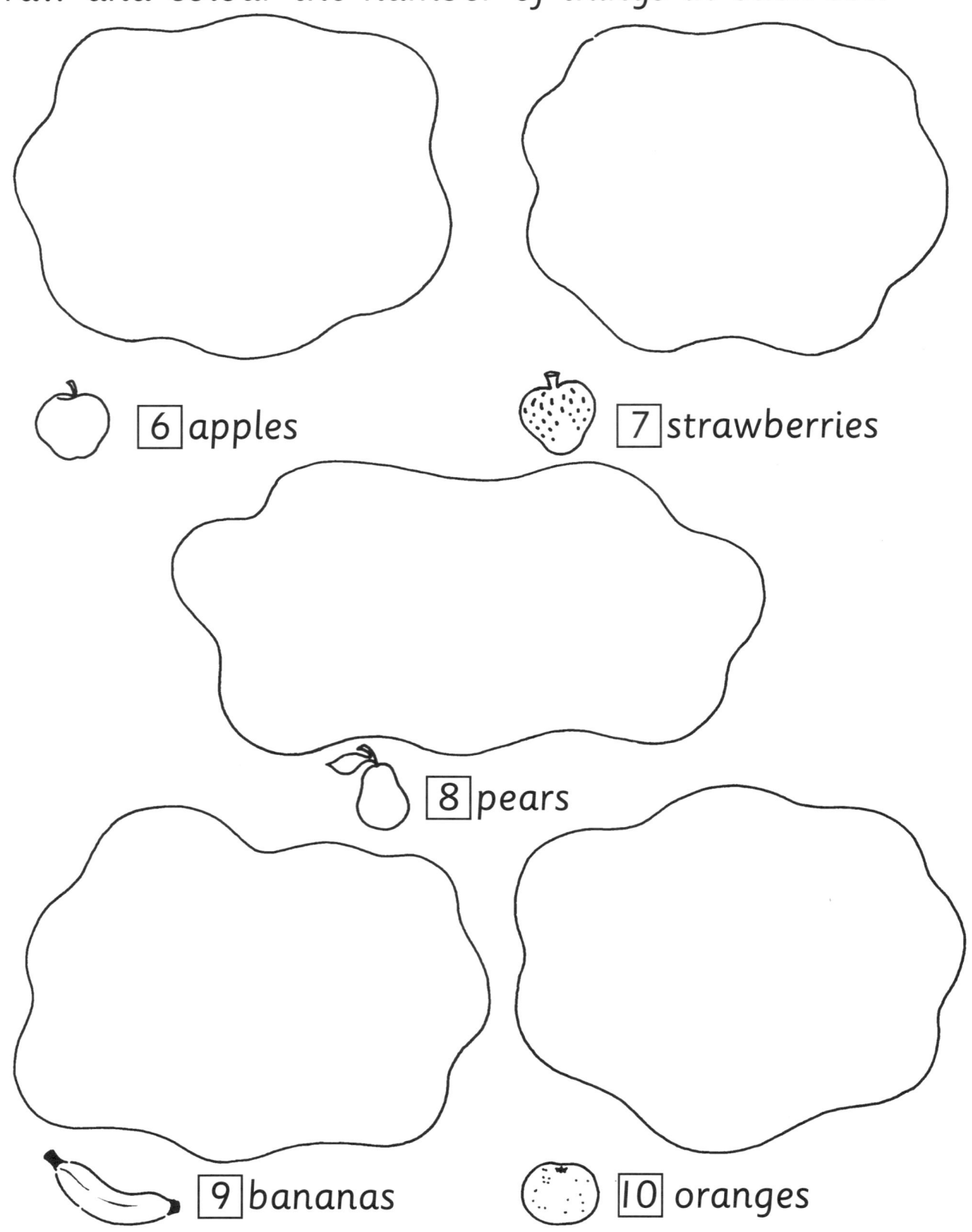

6 apples

7 strawberries

8 pears

9 bananas

10 oranges

Missing numbers 1-5

Counting to 5

Put in the missing numbers.

| 1 | 2 | 3 | 4 | 5 |

19

Times of the day

Starting to tell the time

Write the time in the sentence and put the small hand on the clock at the correct hour.

I get up at _____ o'clock in the morning.

I have my lunch at _____ o'clock in the day.

I go to bed at _____ o'clock at night.

Parent Tip Round times to the nearest hour (o'clock) as this is easiest to learn first. Ask your child to spot the correct hour number on the clock when you say what time he/she does these things.

Dot to dot 1–10

Ordering numbers 1–10

| 1 | 2 | 3 | 4 | 5 | 6 | 7 | 8 | 9 | 10 |

Ordering numbers 1–10

Ordering numbers

| 1 | 2 | 3 | 4 | 5 | 6 | 7 | 8 | 9 | 10 |

Number these beads. Start from the arrow.

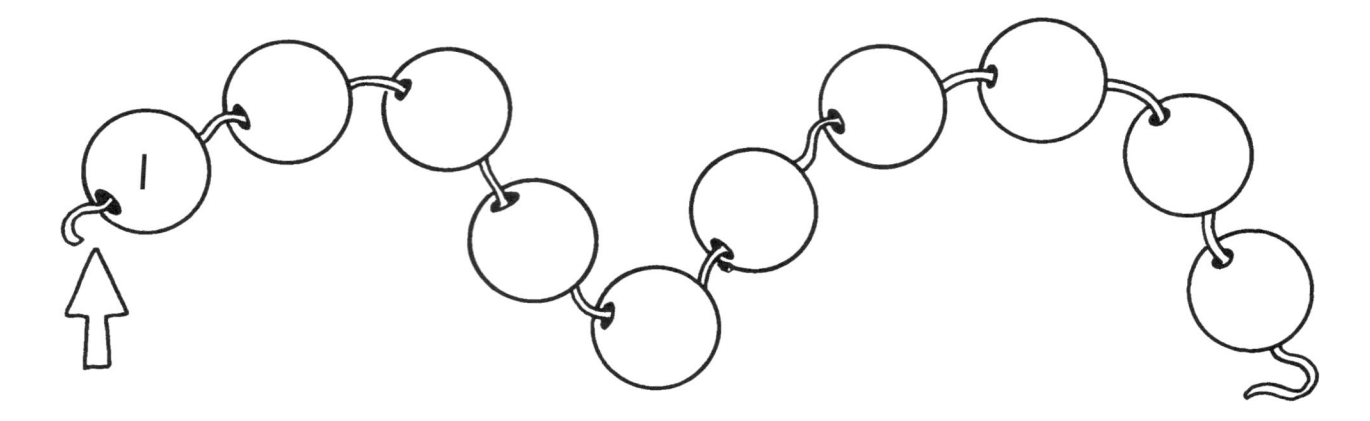

Number these cards. Start with 1 from the dot.

Put the missing numbers on this row of counters.

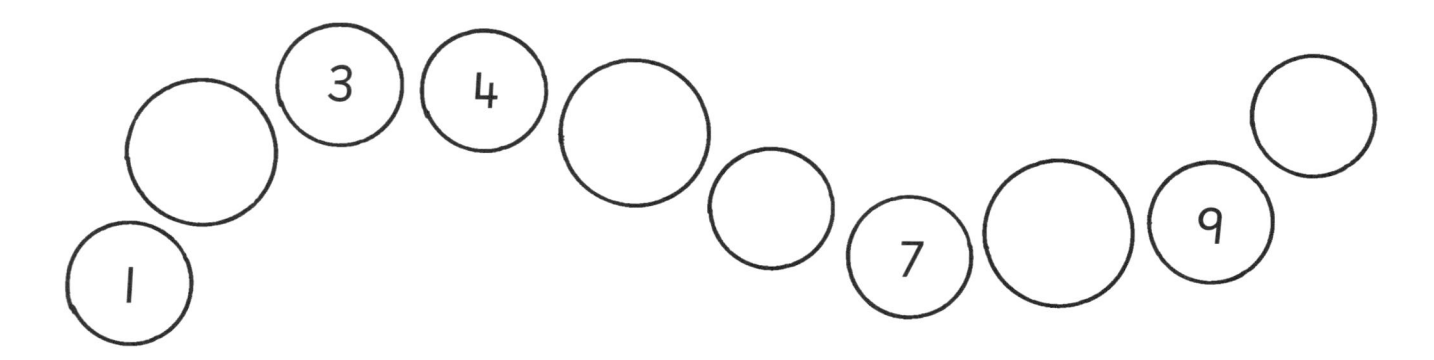

Matching up

Recognising numbers and words

Draw lines to match the dominoes with the correct number and the correct number word.

8   ten

6   seven

10   six

7   eight

9   nine

More than

Bigger and smaller numbers

There are 5 stars on one scarf and 4 stars on the other.
If we match them:

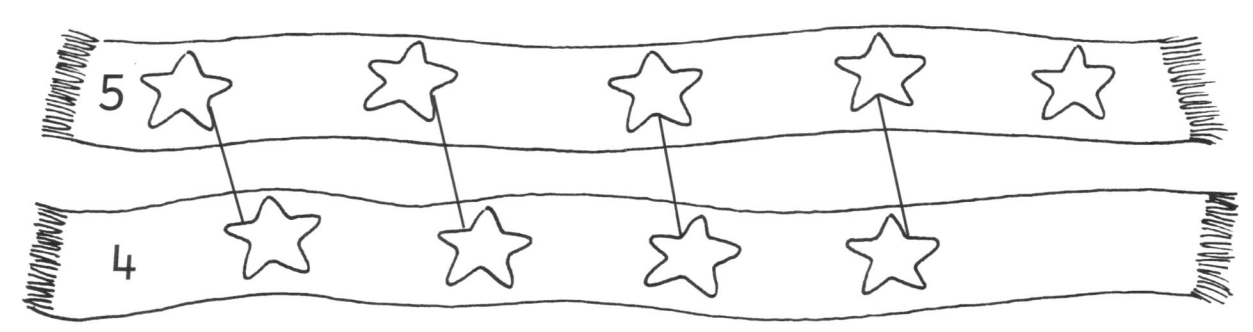

we see that 5 is bigger than 4. It has one more.

☐ 5 ☐ is more than ☐ 4 ☐

Which has more?

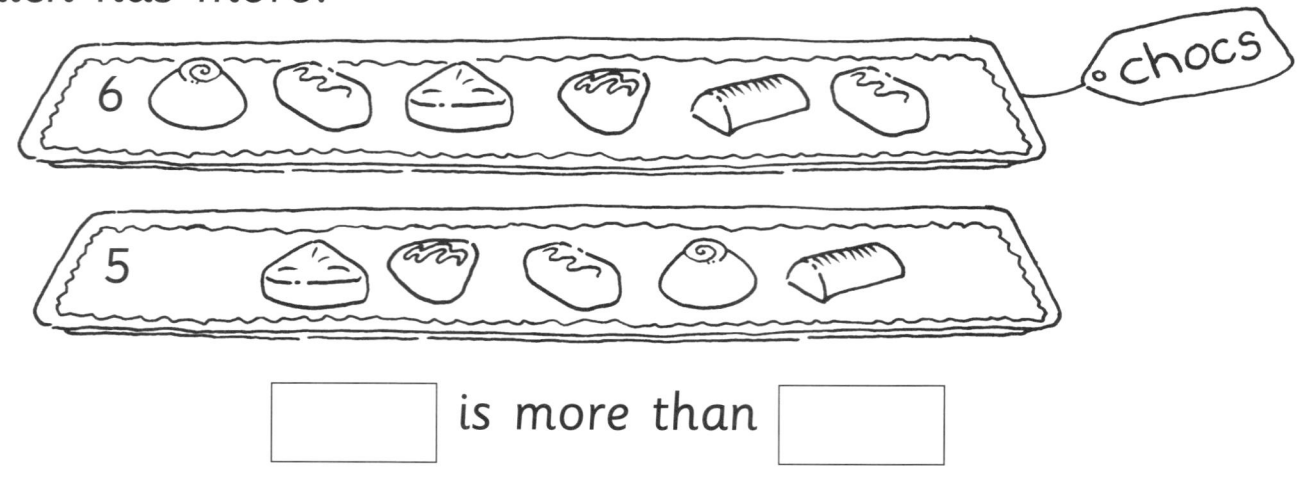

☐ is more than ☐

Which has more?

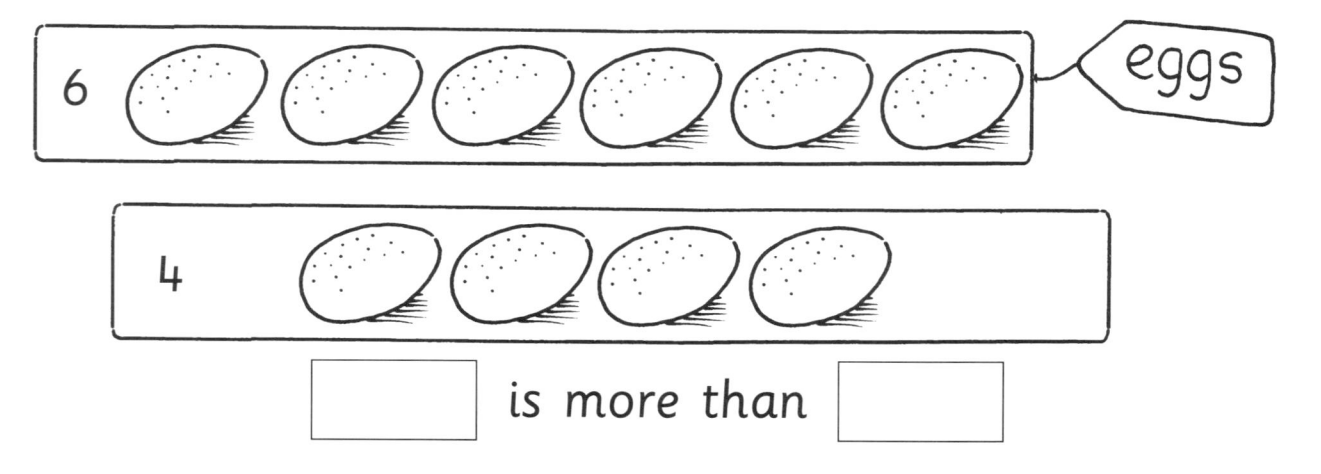

☐ is more than ☐

More and less than

More and less

Colour the bowl which has more fruit red.
Colour the bowl which has less fruit blue.

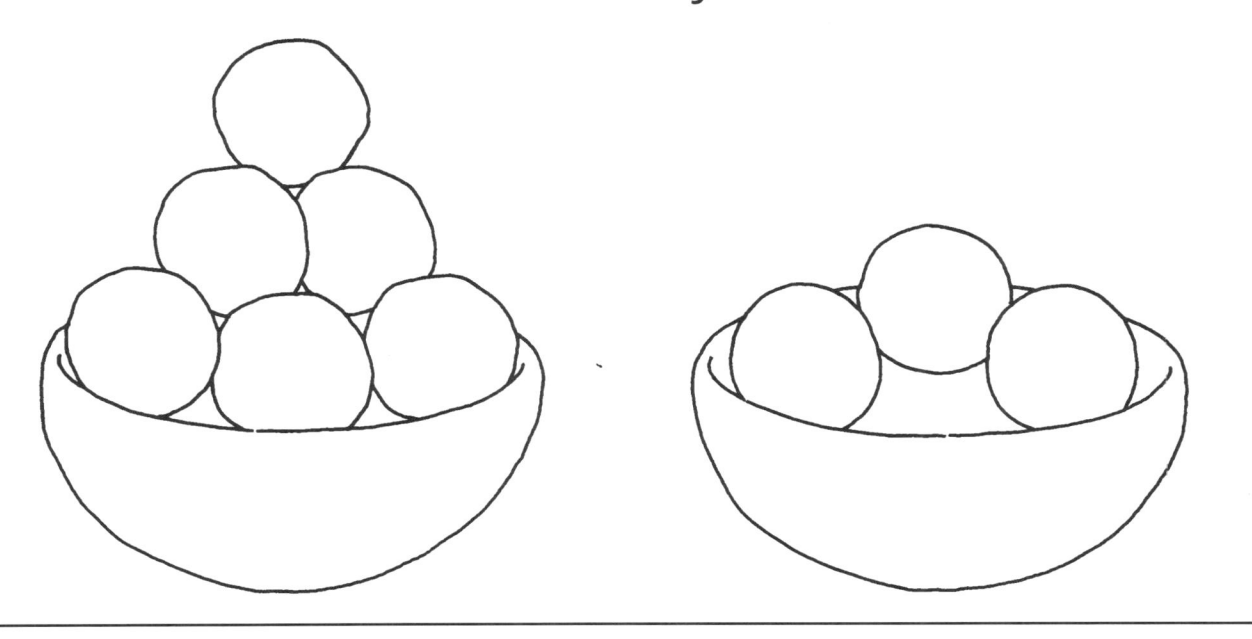

Colour the vase with more flowers yellow.
Colour the vase with less flowers green.

Parent Tip If your child has difficulty with this, do it practically using counters/real fruit/flowers and match one to one as on page 24.

25

Add one more

Simple adding

| 1 | 2 | 3 | 4 | 5 | 6 |

Here are 3 ice creams   Draw 1 more.   How many are there now?

_____

Here are 4 sweets.   Draw 1 more.   How many are there now?

_____

Here are 5 buns.   Draw 1 more.   How many are there now?

_____

Take one away

Sorting shapes and colours

Here are 6 balls.   Take 1 away.   How many are there now?

_____

Here are 5 hats.   Take 1 away.   How many are there now?

_____

Here are 4 coats.   Take 1 away.   How many are there now?

_____

Here are 3 pairs of trousers.   Take 1 away.   How many are there now?

_____

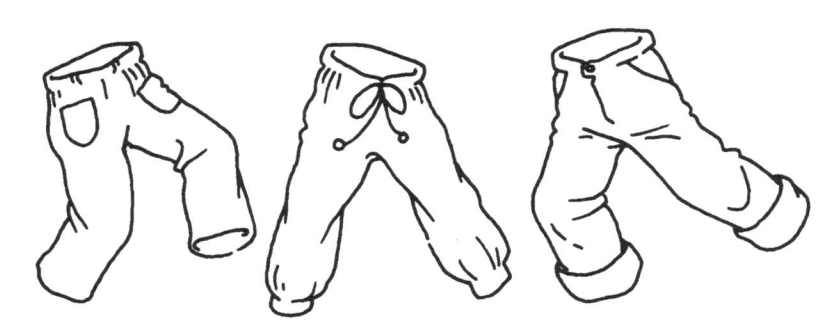

Parent Tip Tell your child to cover one item with a finger to 'take away' (or cross it out with an X), then re-count, leaving out the one item.

Spotting flat shapes

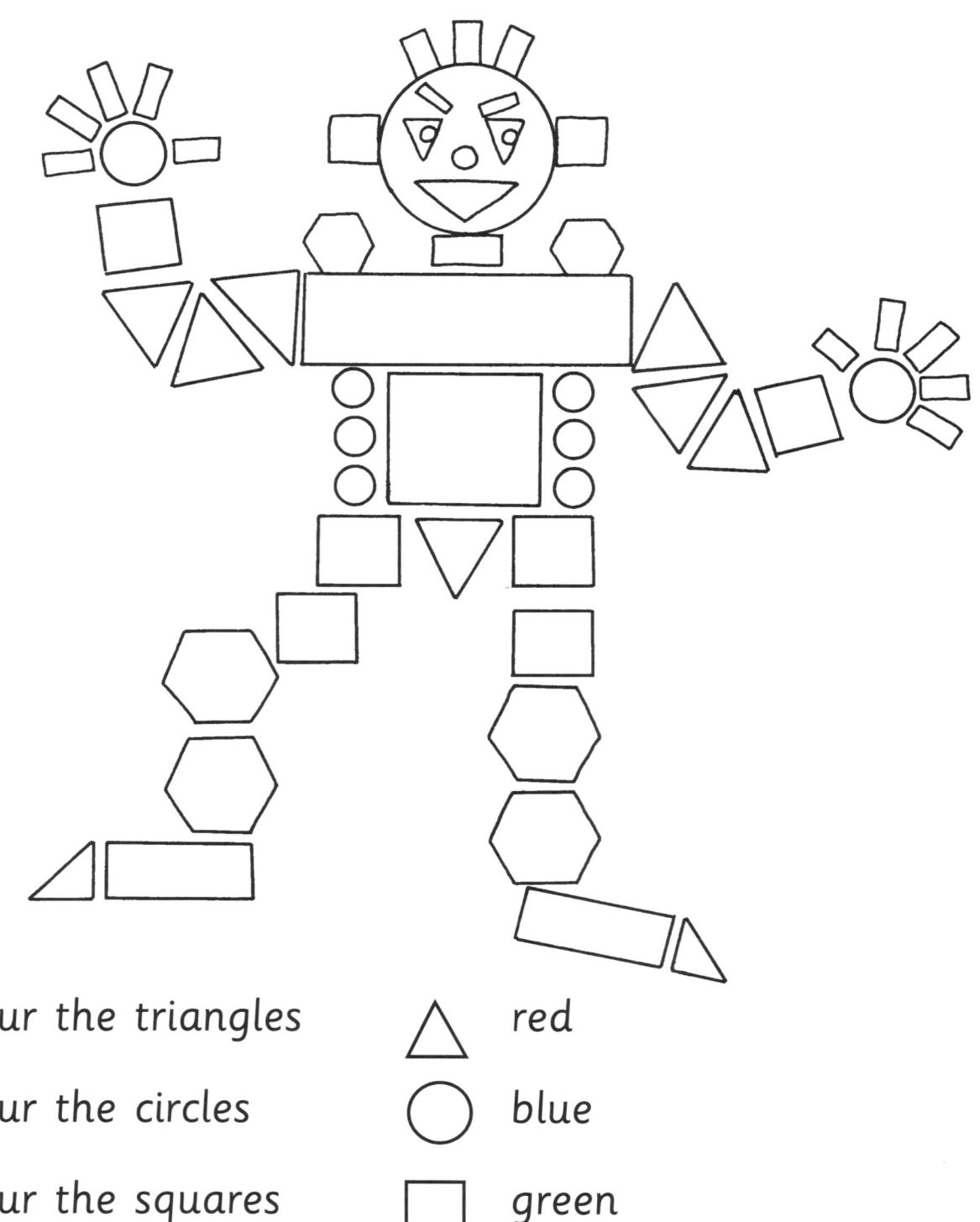

2D shapes

Colour the triangles △ red

Colour the circles ○ blue

Colour the squares □ green

Colour the rectangles ▭ yellow

Colour the hexagons ⬡ orange

Parent Tip Look around the house for these 2D shapes. Use fine pencils to colour this.

Spotting solid shapes

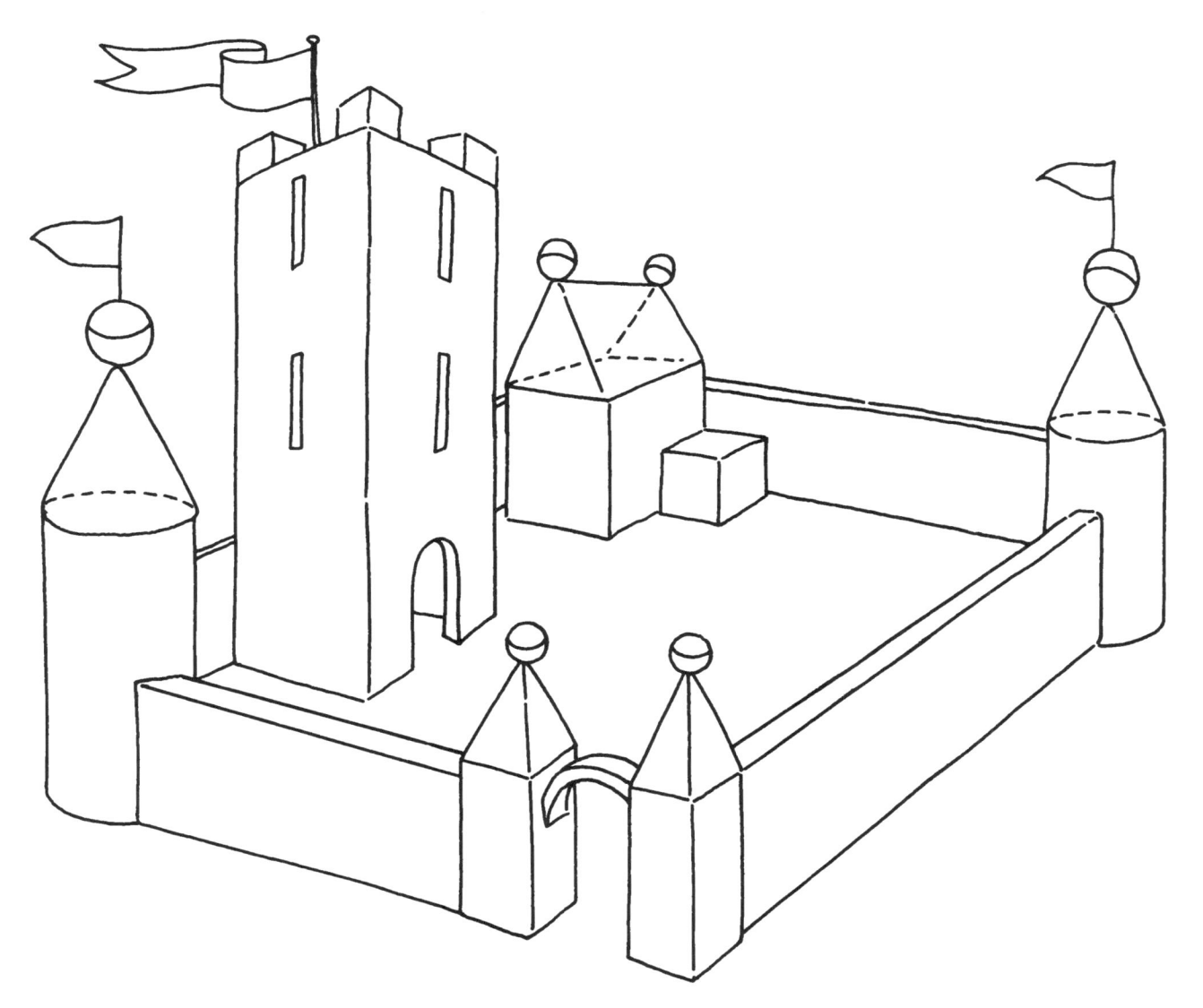

3D shapes

Tick the box if you can see the shape. ✔

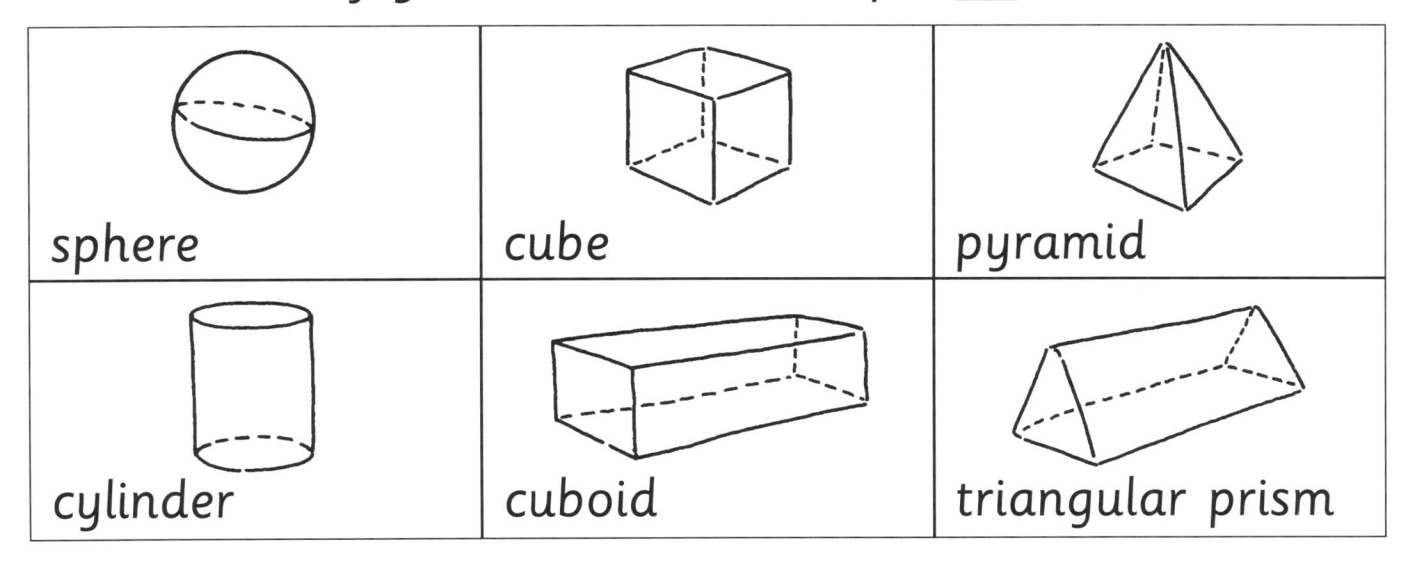

sphere	cube	pyramid
cylinder	cuboid	triangular prism

Parent Tip See if you can find these shapes in the kitchen cupboard!

29

How many altogether?

Simple adding

6 balls

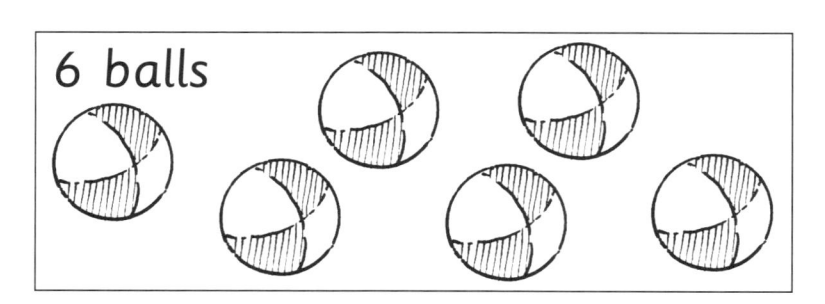

Draw 2 more.

Now there are _____ balls altogether.

7 hats

Draw 1 more.

Now there are _____ hats altogether.

7 cherries

Draw 2 more.

Now there are _____ cherries altogether.

8 lollies

Draw 2 more.

Now there are _____ lollies altogether.

Counting and matching 1–20

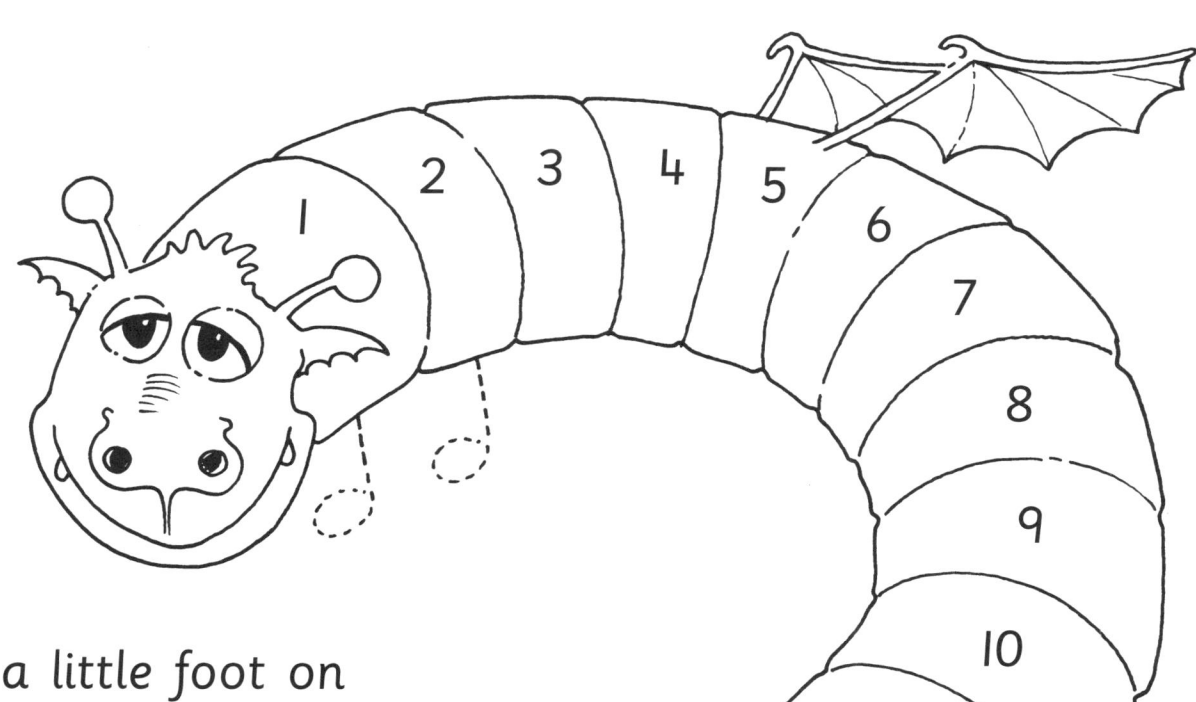

Counting 1–20

Draw a little foot on each piece of Danny Dragon's long body like this: ⇨ ○

He has 20 pieces. Count them, then say the number.

He has 20 buns to eat!

Parent Tip Show your child how to count carefully by saying the number as he/she touches it with his/her finger.

Dot to dot 1–20

Counting 1–20

| 1 | 2 | 3 | 4 | 5 | 6 | 7 | 8 | 9 | 10 |
| 11 | 12 | 13 | 14 | 15 | 16 | 17 | 18 | 19 | 20 |

What am I? Join the dots from 1 to 20 to find out!

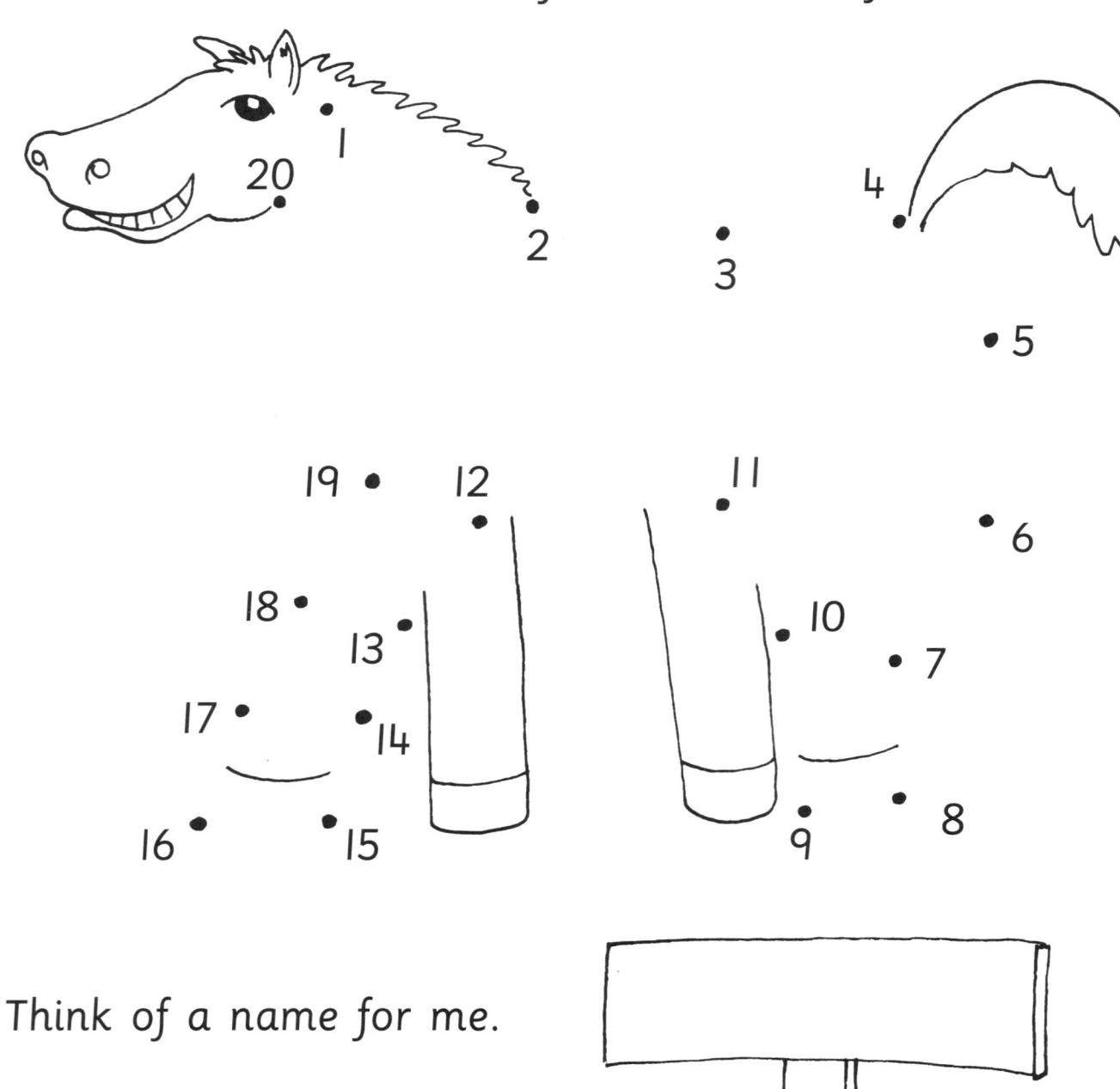

Think of a name for me.

32